RE-FUEL YOUR EMPLOYER BRAND

By James E. Crawley

To CB, whose energy and passion continues to inspire

Refuel Your Employer Brand Copyright © 2018 by James E. Crawley. All Rights Reserved.

All rights reserved. No part of this book may be reproduced in any form or by any electronic or mechanical means including information storage and retrieval systems, without permission in writing from the author. The only exception is by a reviewer, who may quote short excerpts in a review.

Cover designed by James Crawley

James Crawley
Visit my website at www.jcmadvisors.com

Printed in the United States of America

First Printing: September 2018

ISBN – 9781719924337

CONTENTS

About the Author 4
Chapter 1 - Setting the Scene 6
Chapter 2 – Taking Your Pulse 11
Chapter 3 - Setting up Engagement channels 17
Chapter 4 - Corporate Social Responsibility 23
Chapter 5 - Appraising your organisation 30
Chapter 6 - Let's Talk About Flexibility 33
Chapter 7 - Using Social Media. 37
Chapter 8 - Communication Communication Communication! 40
Chapter 9 – Recruitment 42
Chapter 9 ¾ - The True Costs of Recruitment 67
Chapter 10 – The Recruitment Process 70
Chapter 11 – References 75
Chapter 12 – Other Tools and Their Value in Creating your Employer Brand 79
Chapter 13 – Your HR Department Is Not Your Recruitment Department 85
Chapter 14   Ownership 88
Chapter 15 – Good People Are Leaving. Is My Employer Brand Broken? 91
Chapter 16 – Three Pillars of Creating a Killer Employer Brand 93
Chapter 17 – Conclusions 95

By James E. Crawley

About the Author

James started his professional life as a submariner in the Royal Navy, possibly the best free management training school in the world. After a few very enjoyable years, he decided that seeing further than ten feet occasionally would be nice, and some daylight wouldn't go amiss either. So, he packed his bags, and after an eighteen-month notice period, set off from the Barrow-In-Furness submarine building centre in search of his wife, whom he had last spotted in Kent in a house he vaguely remembered buying. He, having met a few head hunters on his own job search, fell into the world of executive search, started as a researcher and worked his way up.

Two start-ups, two turnarounds, a PLC, a venture capital backed rocket ship of company later, one divorce, the installation of wife v2.0 + with two preinstalled apps and an awful lot of fun later, James found that he had transitioned from a pure exec search consultant into a broad business consultant with a focus on talent. Somehow twenty years had passed and realising that no existing company would work the way he wanted it to, he launched JCM Advisors (JCM), an international talent management and business consulting firm. In 2018, launching JCM Management Advisors with his brother and JCM Medical Advisors (having found he had a spare 30 minutes one Monday morning) , he renamed JCM Advisors to JCM Advisors Group and separated out JCM Talent Advisors as a distinct brand.

Still working with the leadership teams of some of the world's top professional services firms, who were clients that have been loyal for nearly two decades, the core mission for JCM is now to help smaller faster growing companies learn from their predecessors' mistakes.

Whilst still maintaining a London presence, James tries to hide away in Kent when not on active engagements. He also spends thirty percent of his time working with local and national charities ranging from The British Red Cross to SouthEast4x4 response. He is also the Lead Governor of South East Coast Ambulance Service and a Community First Responder.

By James E. Crawley

Chapter 1 – Setting the Scene

My first book introduced the concept of fuelling your employer brand. After it was published, and I had discussed it with Peers, Business Leaders and Owners, a wealth of additional information emerged. This led to a number of research projects that catalysed and developed my thinking around the Employer Brand concept. Fuel Your Employer Brand really looked at the very basic concepts of the subject, and whilst it covered many aspects of the topic it also delved very heavily into the subject of recruitment process, as having a strong recruitment process is one of the foundation blocks of building a sustainable employer brand.

This book therefore takes the original chapters of the first book that are most relevant and builds on them. You could therefore consider this the second edition, however there is so much additional content I decided that the content was significant enough to warrant its own separate publication. Perhaps "Fuel Your Employer Brand "could be considered the beginners guide, and this the more advanced source of advice for those that have created a good Employer Brand and now want to take it to the next level.

When it comes to Employee Engagement it always fascinates me how wide the gulf often is between the CEO/Boards/Owners understanding of a situation and the reality of what the staff are feeling. Sometimes there can be an over reliance on staff surveys and happiness dashboards and often not enough time spent on the front line.

Don't get me wrong, we use tools such as Engagement Multiplier and they are very powerful tools, but these are all active methods that rely on people answering surveys in a consistent and accurate manner. They provide a baseline to work to but they do not provide the ultimate answer.

The trick, we believe, is to interpret this data but then add in passive sources such as keeping up to date with your organisations internal social feeds, have tools such as an anonymous suggestion boxes ,where in our experience, people are generally more open and honest.

Once informed, senior management need to get out on the ground, and spend "quality time" with no fixed agenda with their teams. Too often organisations rely on "town halls" or pre-planned engagement events.

Whilst these are effective at transmitting messages, they are very poor for receiving them. Colleagues will often avoid suggesting things out in the open for fear highlighting themselves if the suggestion is deemed inappropriate.

Employee Engagement matters, as it directly impacts your growth, your stability, your customers and your products. Refuelling your employer brand should be a constant evolving project in your business. Whether a start-up or an established business of either local or global proportions, its equally relevant to you. Like "Fuel Your Employer Brand" this book is for the business leader or the individual responsible for talent, rather than the HR professional, who will already be well acquainted with this subject.

Steve Jobs once said, 'Marketing is about values...... it's a very noisy world ...we are not going to get a chance to get people to remember much about us, no company is.....Apple is one of half a dozen best brands in the whole world......but even a great brand needs investment and caring if it's going to retain its relevance and vitality'. Mr Jobs was talking about the product, but I would hypothesise that the same principles apply to talent acquisition as well. Without marketing, you cannot create a brand, and without a brand, you can't attract talent, well not without overpaying for it anyway.

So, the principles laid out in this book revolve around how you can create and protect that brand – your employer brand.

Just today I came across an advertisement from a leading consumer brand, PepsiCo. The following is what they were looking for:

> 'We're hiring a Director to lead PepsiCo's Global Attraction & Engagement function, which includes elevating our employer brand through external digital and social channels and collaborating with our talented teams across the globe to share transparent & inspiring stories. Join us in showcasing what makes PepsiCo unique through the lens and voice of our employees on global and local platforms, in a differentiating and inspiring way'.

Employer Branding is now a function. 20 years ago, they might have been asking for a 'Director of Recruitment' or 'Recruitment Manager'; now attracting people to jobs is as big as attracting customers to a business. From people comes product, and if you don't have the right people, you won't have the right product.

Sandy Asch, author of the fantastic *Excellence at Work – The Six Keys to Inspire Passion in the Workplace,* laid out six key things that employers can do to become an employer of choice if they were adopted by everyone in the organisation from the top down. They are as follows:

> **Use your word wisely.** It is important to communicate with employees with honesty, openness and respect. Communications should focus on what is possible.
>
> **Be accountable.** Employers should act proactively and be committed to truth-telling, focusing on the question behind the question rather than offering excuses or explanations.
>
> **Focus.** By focusing on independent goals, employers can extract the greatest value from the efforts of employees.
>
> **Mine the gold.** Employees and managers should strive to bring out the best in their employees and be committed to collaboration and cooperation.
>
> **Strive for balance.** Employees will be vital and energetic at work as a result of a balanced life. Employers should, therefore, give their employees the opportunity to refresh and renew.
>
> **Lighten up.** Perhaps the most difficult of the six principles, employees should not take themselves very seriously. Employers and their employees should seek to bring laughter and joy to the workplace and look for opportunities to make other's day.

I think Asch is spot on, and I don't disagree with any of these points. These principles, however, apply mainly to those individuals already through the door. This book explores employer brand from an earlier starting point – the start of the recruitment lifecycle.

We are going to cover taking the "pulse" of the organisation, how to create basic employee engagement models, how to set up your corporate social responsibility agenda and how to make all of that count whether you are a new start-up or a global organisation.

I am a very practical person, and all the advice contained within, therefore, is of a practical rather than theoretical nature; it is gained from two decades of making mistakes and watching other people make mistakes from large blue-chip environments to one-person start-ups.

If the book resonates with you, please get in touch. If it doesn't, well at least you have somewhere to put your coffee cup down now if you bought the hard copy.

If you are reading this on your phone, then I have a recommendation for you before you read on. Go to YouTube and type in 'Gary Turk – Look Up'.

Chapter 2 – Taking Your Pulse

It's very hard to fix an organisation's employer brand if the organization doesn't know what that brand currently is. I often find clients have some sort of methodology in place, but it's rarely comprehensive and even more rarely does cover all the elements it needs to, nor is it consistently applied. Like a piece of half cooked chicken on the BBQ you may be ok, but equally you may end up giving the organisation the equivalent of food poisoning by acting on partial information. You had the best of intentions by quickly collating the information, but the road to the talent desert is tarmacked with good intentions.

Let's look at some of the most popular methods companies use to ascertain how well their organisation is doing.

Exit Interviews

Pro's: Exit interviews are extremely valuable sources of information. Exiting employees are generally more reticent than exiting employees to give accurate negative feedback for fear of impacting their own careers, so you can glean some useful nuggets of information.

Cons: How tainted the view you receive from the employee is wholly depends on the circumstances of their exit. Do they have an axe to grind with their previous managers, were they dissatisfied with their role, their career prospects, their rewards. Beware the lone "exiter" who may decide to pull the pin and throw the grenade on the way out.

This methodology more than any other demonstrates the danger of relying on a sole source of information.

Surveys

Surveys can take many forms, can be done at a variety of intervals and can provide a useful source of information. There are many tools out there, probably the most popular of which is "Survey Monkey" (if you do use survey monkey, please please please have the nous to pay for the paid version rather than use the free version. Nothing says "I don't really care about this, but I have to do it" to your employees than using free tools for employee engagement.

Pros
Generally they can be set up to be anonymous (remind me later to explain why you shouldn't need these to be anonymous), and therefore the accuracy of answers is generally quite high. They can be easily tailored to the both organisation, but also to changing circumstances. They are quick and easy to complete, and the results are instantaneous.

Cons

A survey is only ever as good as the questions it asks. Surveys that are too long have low compliance rates and surveys that are too short can often be conceived as unimportant.

Suggestion Boxes

A very useful tool in any type of organisation. Whilst they are often literally physical boxes, these days there are virtual versions such as www.suggestionox.com which are extremely valuable in virtual or multisite operations.

Pros: Easy to set up, passive ways of collecting ideas for your organisation or for product development
Cons: Doesn't actually tell you anything about the mood of culture in your organisation. Just because you are getting lots of suggestions doesn't mean your organisation is either happy or sad.

Entry Interviews

A rarely used, valuable tool that speaks volumes about your external perception by candidates.
Pros: Untainted fresh views from a fresh pair of eyes in to the organisation.
Cons: Limited scope of views, will a new employee really be an accurate critical eye?

Staff Appraisals

Now of course you are all going to say "we do these already" and maybe you do. More likely than not you will indeed sit down once a year and discuss the performance of a member of staff, their aspirations, maybe their training needs going forward. How many of you do a full 360 degree appraisal where there the staff appraise the management and the business and the product?

Pros: Detailed feedback from staff who know what they are talking about. If applied consistently across the organisation, then a bank of data can be collated which can then be analysed for consistent themes and issues.
Cons: Relies on a very open management style to get accurate results.

In Summary

All of these methods have value, but that value is limited unless more than one method is used. We use a tool called "Engagement Multiplier" (https://www.engagementmultiplier.com/partner/jcm/) with our client which is a comprehensive tool that encompasses many of the methods about, however we don't use it in isolation. Analytics can only tell you so much, sometimes you have to sit in the room with someone and rely on the mark one eyeball to really understand what they are saying. We take the results of EM, which are largely anonymous unless otherwise selected, but we follow that up with one to one interviews / conversations with the client's teams to validate that data.

The other most important aspect of this activity is visibility. Publish the results. So many management teams use these methods then try and present an edited version of positive highlights. People know what they wrote and said, they probably have a pretty good idea what their colleagues wrote and said, so if you try and wrap up in glitter they will see straight through it and the credibility of the exercise is destroyed in an instant.

Management failure is not when an organisation makes a mistake. Management failure is when an organisation fails to recognise the mistakes it has made. Transparency is key, and I think you will find will be welcomed by your team who will respect the guts it takes to be this honest about yourself and your business.

I said remind me to tell you why the word "anonymous" should be a dirty word in your organisation. The only reason a member of your team should feel the need to say something to you anonymously is if they live in fear of reprisals. Now I am pretty sure you don't want to run an organisation on fear. It's hardly the healthiest, most productive of environments is it? Maybe it's a perception of fear that doesn't really exist, either way you have a problem because until you fix this you have very little chance of improving the overall culture.

An organisations culture should be open, honest and embrace challenges. Good leaders should never be afraid to receive honest feedback and should thank the team members who care enough about the organisation to criticise it in a positive way. In the Navy, the "lower deck" as it was called, or in other words the shop floor where the work is actually be done always grumbles. Grumbles are ok, its when it goes silent as you walk past you need to worry!

Now I am great believer in keeping things simple, and this is where something like survey monkey can be really valuable, why don't you use to ask your team how they would like to be engaged. Ask them directly would they prefer an anonymous approach or a more open approach. Whatever the answer you have at least established a baseline to work from and can identity whether you have an open or a closed culture.

Chapter 3 – Setting up Engagement channels

Clearly the size of your organisation will dictate to some degree the engagement model you might like to adopt. If you are a 5-person company, having engagement champions, staff engagement forums, partnership meetings etc may be considered more than a little excessive. However, if you are a company on a growth curve, its much easier to put the structures in place now that grow with you than try to impose new structures once you have grown. I would suggest therefore that there are steps that any company can put in place, and then additional steps that can be pre planned to activate as the company reaches a certain size. I shall divide this chapter into three then, starting small (in terms of people not revenue) ad then growing to large.

Small Companies

We are talking here about companies that are 5-50 people and run on a single site. (If you run a company of less than 5 people and are having to read this book for advice on how to engage with your people then may I suggest that a) You choose another career other than entrepreneur or company owner or b) go give yourself a dammed good talking to in front of the mirror)

In companies this size, what generally happens is that the owners or leaders try to run the business the same way as when it was a handful of people. They forget that they don't have the same amount of time as they did to spend with individual members of staff. If a member of staff isn't causing any issues then they tend to get forgotten and the focus of the business owner is on the more problematic staff members. This is a critical mistake that leads to the most loyal staff members eventually becoming dissatisfied and leaving - usually to the great surprise of the owners who thought they could rely on this person. It doesn't matter how loyal a member of your team is, if they don't perceive they are being valued or even worse perceive they are being taken advantage of because they are diligent and dedicated and capable, eventually they will find a new path.

What I suggest to clients who are this size is keep it simple but make it scalable. In an organisation of over 5 people there will be some sort of hierarchy and therefore there will be a body of people who are the management and a body of people who are the team. Here are some simple ideas you can implement at this scale:

- Ask your team what engagement they would like

- Ask your team if they would like to choose a member of the team to come to relevant sections of management meetings to represent the team and provide a two-way communication channel

- Keep your team informed of developments in the business. I would recommend as a minimum a quarterly company meeting where the management team discuss the performance and plans for the business and seek input from the team

- Annually, be completely transparent about the results of the company and the earnings of the directors. This information is generally easy to find out anyway, and by being open with it, it can help develop a culture of openness in the organisation. It also provides an aspiration point for individuals in the business who are motivated and ambitious.
- Run at least two surveys a year of your staff on all aspects of the business (or use a continue assessment tool such as Engagement Manager)
- Set up some form of suggestion box tool, physical or virtual that is easy for the team to access. This should ideally be open so that staff can be recognised for their ideas, but could also be anonymous using something like suggestionOx.

Medium Sized Companies

Now we are talking 50-5,000 people, maybe on one site but more likely spread across different geographies either nationally or internationally. Clearly with this sized business we should start seeing strong management structures in place. Departmental structures might be starting to form, site specific structures might also start to become relevant, which will serve the business well, but the organisation may not yet have the talent structure in place to serve the people well.

In addition to the above steps we now need to start building in some additional layers.

- Every department or site should have a staff engagement champion, ideally voted into the role by the members of that team. This individual should be given protected time away from their core role to enable to them to fulfil the role and dedicate the necessary time.
- If your company is more than 1,000 people you probably want to start thinking about employing a staff engagement professional on a full time basis who will guide and work with the staff champions.
- All the staff champions in the business should have a regular meetings / conversations with their team to get their feedback and ideas and promulgate management ideas. They should have a joint meeting with other champions and key executives to exchange these ideas.
- Where a company has a multisite operation, executives need to rota themselves to conduct informal drop in sessions at remote sites so that staff don't suffer from the head office/local office mindset.

- Some people think that awards ceremonies are a bit twee. I don't, I think done right they can be very powerful in recognising employee achievement without just relying on the pay packet. A company of this size should have some recognition scheme in place for things such as

    o Best Innovative Idea
    o Best Customer Feedback
    o Long Service awards

I would avoid "Best Deal, Top Biller" type awards because salespeople are quite self-motivating and well rewarded for their roles. At the end of the day if someone is the top salesmen then they are doing what you are paying them to do, but if someone has an amazing idea then that should be recognised. I watched a program on TV the other day about a sausage factory. In the packing line the packers would stand on one side of the table putting sausages that came down a chute into plastic cartons. One day one of the packers, who used to be an engineer, had the idea to have a moving arm on the chute that pushed the sausages to either side of the packing table which enabled the company to put packers on both side an increased packing capacity by 40%. That's the sort of engagement and innovation you want to both engender but also celebrate.

- Perks. When a company reaches a certain size, things like healthcare plans, additional pension contributions start appearing in peoples packages. Nothing wrong with this but they become the expected norm and therefore don't shift the engagement score of an organisation very much. However if there are some perks to being part of an organisation that are useful on a day to day basis then these can start to have quite a significant impact

- With this size of organisation if you haven't done so already you might want to start to think about employee participation in the ownership of the company. There are many models to think about from sweet equity through to share options. It's a very personal decision and I am not going to lecture any entrepreneur on what they should do in this regard. All I will say is that employees with some skin in the game are generally considerably more motivated to the long term success of the company.

Larger Companies

5,000 plus people, multisite, National and International companies would fall into this category. If you have already put in place the steps above on your growth journey then guess what, you just need to scale up what you already have. In my decades of business what I have consistently found is that the growth from small to medium is time consuming, challenging, frustrating but ultimately rewarding. If you put in place the outline of structures as you go along, when you try to go from medium to large the journey is much simpler. If you haven't put in place the small and medium steps yet, then go hire yourself a engagement specialist who can rapidly ramp up this aspect of your management structure.

Chapter 4 – Corporate Social Responsibility

CSR started to rise to prominence in the 1960's, but really got into its stride in the 1990's with Generation X, was developed further with Generation Y, but really has become vital any organisation with Millennial's.

Initially conceived largely as a marketing tool, it became a way for brands to show how nice they were, and ranged from Charitable donations to international causes to staff donating their and the companies time to local projects or causes. The "donations" generated publicity for the companies both in terms of customer and employer brand.

The thing is, the impact on Employer Brand (how attractive your organisation is to external talent looking to join), of these activities is now massively diminished because not only has everyone else caught up, the younger generations genuinely care more about topics and judge potential employers on their actions more than ever before. These large scale "foundations" however are largely perceived as corporate tax break schemes with little true genuine feeling or passion for the subject matter. When I tell you that a well known coffee company donates just .01% to their foundation despite plastering it over the walls of every store you get some idea of what I am on about. Now there are of course exceptions and there are some companies set up as not for profit social enterprises , and these should be applauded. In this book we are aiming more for the Charles Montgomery Burns's of this world than the Bill and Melinda Gates's.

I have spent the last few months interviewing young people, entrepreneurs and business leaders about their view on CSR both as an Employer and as a potential employee. Several things became clear about this, but the most interesting thing was what I call the care curve.

When we are born and go through childhood, at some point we become cognisant of "causes" be they political, environmental, societal etc, and as we enter our teenage years these often become more important and seem to peak in most people in their mid 20's. As we progress towards middle age we seem to care slightly less about these "causes" probably because this coincides with when most people start settling down and having families and priorities become more practical. It certainly reaches a rock bottom point in peoples 40's (note this is an average generalisation, clearly a minority of people believe so passionately about a cause they make it their entire life). Then at some point in peoples 40's, maybe they feel secure and stable, they start caring more again and start making lifestyle and career choices not only on financial or practical aspects but also on company ethics and values - just as passionately, if not more, as they did when they left school, college or university.

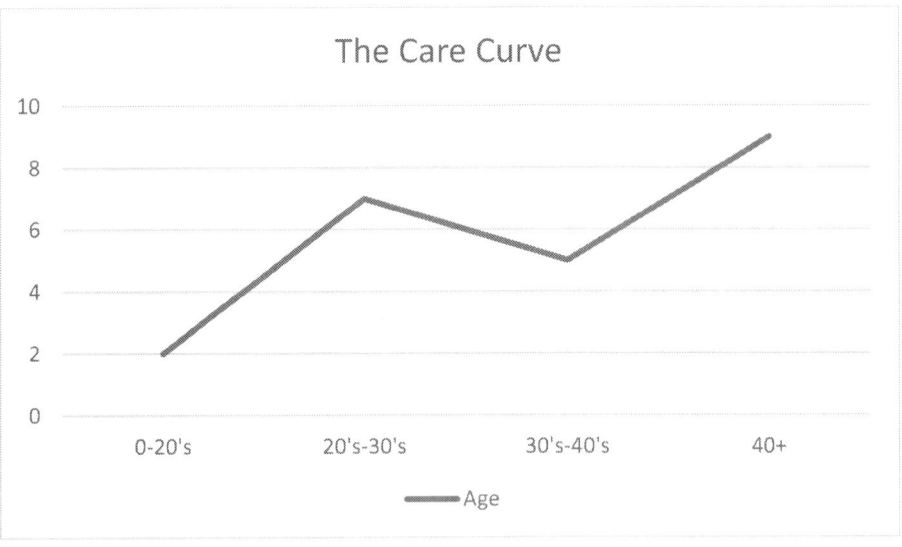

This is very important for employers when considering their employer brand in today's world. Whether you are looking to attract fresh graduates or experienced team members and executives, all these groups will look to your CSR agenda and assess it on several points:

a) Is it genuine? - if you are giving away less than .01% of your profits in effort or money then no one is going to believe you have any serious commitment to positively changing the environment you operate in.

b) Is it relevant? - if you are a bottled water company that gives back by digging wells in Africa that is relevant. If you are a local estate agent donating to the local football or rugby team, that's not relevant. In fact, that is not even CSR that will affect your employees, that's marketing or spend on customer service.

c) Is it effective? - CSR is only valuable if it makes a difference, and it will only positively impact and fuel your employer brand if the results are demonstrable to your potential audience, be that employees or customers.

I often get asked what a good level of "contribution" makes a difference to CSR and the answer is I don't know. JCM Advisors gives away 30 % of its efforts to not for profits, other firms give away less than 1%. The answer is it's up to you. CSR should be core to your values, and if your values are strong then your CSR should reflect those values.

Like most things in life it will only happen if you commit to it and put some effort it. As Terry's say about their chocolate oranges "whack it don't tap it"

So What Is CSR?

So now you have some understanding of the importance of CSR, you might be wondering what it actually is. Ask a lot of people what CSR is and they might well say "It's companies giving back to their local communities", or "it's companies being conscientious recyclers in their office" My definition of CSR is this:

"Corporate Social Responsibility involves any impact a company has on its people, the environment in which it operates and the environment where its products have an impact"

So basically, anything can fit within the definition of CSR. What you need to decide is what your values are and therefore what CSR is going to mean to you, your people and your customers. Here are some key elements you will want to include:

- Investment in Social Issues in your local geographic area
- Investment in Suppliers / Producers wellbeing.
- Investment in Employee Development
- Investment in Employee Wellbeing
- Investment in Minimising Your Environmental Impact
- Investment in customer service

We recently ran a survey of business owners, SME's through to blue chip international companies, and asked these owners what priority they would invest in each of the above topics. We then averaged weighted the answers and got some interesting results:

As you can see most employers claimed that investment in employees was very high on their spend agenda, however the fact that Investment in customer service features quite so strongly I would suggest is a worry. Why should a company be investing in Customer Service at all?

That may sound a bit strange – surely every company should invest in customer service? Well no, they shouldn't, and I will tell you why. If you invest all your available resources into your people, then your people will take care of customer services automatically. If you are having to spend additional resources specifically on customer services, then you have a customer service issue which means you are having to reward customers who complain.

How?

So how do you develop your CSR agenda? Well, being conscientious observers of the advice in this book, you already have the ideal forum in which to start developing these ideas – your team, whether via the engagement champions if you are a medium or larger business or through the regular meetings you are now having with your team. Ask your team what's important to them, even ask your customers.

When you have answered that you can start to make plans. Often a business leader will have a personal cause or charity they like to support – that's fine, but don't let that become the be all and end all of your CSR Agenda. You might like to support the hospice that looked after your relative so well, but if half your team like dogs more than humans, you might like to look at an animal shelter as well for the charitable donations element of your programme. There is no "one size fits all" model, every business is different and therefore every CSR program should be different.

Some core principals I personally like to adopt are:

- Allocate sufficient resource for success to be realistic

- Try and make the CSR agenda adopt both company's aims and personal aims. For example, if you are giving each employee 3 days annually for CSR work with charities then make at least one of those days a company "team" CSR day where you do something together, but let the employee choose which charity to donate their remaining time to

- Let your team decide what development programmes, courses etc they want to do. Do NOT mix up your CSR programme with your companies vocational training programme. Mandatory training is not CSR. When we talk about investing in employee's development we mean additional skills that make them a better rounded individual, not a better car mechanic or management consultant. It doesn't matter if the course is butterfly photography, if that is what they want to do.

- Employee wellbeing is very difficult to encapsulate for all your employees as their needs will vary wildly. I would suggest providing some taster sessions for some obvious ones such as Mindfulness, Lunchtime Yoga, Cycle to Work Scheme (don't forget employees need somewhere to shower and change!) , Gym memberships etc and see what gets adopted. Again, ask people what they would like to try and be conscious of any implications such as Tax Implications

Chapter 5 – Appraising your organisation

So how do you currently go about appraising your organisation and your people? Do you do annual appraisals, performance development reviews, annual assessments of any other name or type. If you have a successful business I am sure that you do. Your probably sit down with your team regularly and discuss their contribution to the business, set their targets, discuss their bonuses etc. Well done, give yourself a nice pat on the back, that's a good start. If you don't, stop reading here, do the above and then come back and read the rest of this book when you are running your business properly.

How many of you are regularly asking your team how well the business is being run in a formal way? Not so many, I thought so. It's quite a brave thing to do for the Managing Director of a multi-million-pound business to ask the employee on the loading dock what he thinks of the management. But you know what? The employee on the loading dock has probably spotted that the trucks are being loaded in the wrong order long before the management see it. Remember the sausage factory? It wasn't a member of the management team or an external consultant that improved productivity on the packing line by 40% in an instant, it was a member of the team who worked on the packing line.

I don't care if you are a law firm, sausage manufacturer or a hospital, the same principles apply. The answers to most of your problems are probably already contained within the "brain trust" of your organisation. You just need to find a way to extract it.

I am very certain that leadership of an organisation is more important than management. With good leadership, many people will manage themselves as empowered employees, so if you have an open culture that allows from appraisals upwards as well as downwards, I genuinely feel that you will ultimately be more successful. That's why, I believe, truly great organisations have great Leaders not Managers as CEO's.

So, appraisals then. Yes, they should focus on the employee, their performance and their development needs but they should also have a strong section on performance of the business and the management of the business.

I never understand why bosses are so afraid to do this? At the end of the day it's about receiving the messages, its not always about acting on them. Whilst only a fool wouldn't actively listen to his team, it doesn't mean the team is right. The act of listening and being open to ideas and criticism is the important thing here, not ultimately acting on every single suggestion.

Don't believe me? How come "Back to the floor" or "Undercover Boss" are such popular TV programmes, in fact Emmy Award winning programmes? I can't find a single example of a "Boss" who has appeared on this show and regretted it. If there is any regret to be had its from the Boss during the show who can't believe that the feedback they are getting hasn't made it to the board room before.

What "bosses" get from this experience is unadulterated feedback from the people that matter. Now you don't need to put on a John Lennon wig and Elton John glasses and go and hang around the watercooler to receive these messages, you need an accurate 360-degree appraisal programme.

Chapter 6 – Let's Talk About Flexibility

No, I don't mean Yoga obviously, that's dangerous and you can hurt yourself and falls under my life categories of don't go there if you weigh 120kg.

I read an interesting Forbes.com article recently about how CEOs in America are struggling to cope with professionals that have dual-career households.   It made the point that most policies and procedures in established organisation predicated one "dominant" earner in the household.   So, companies have good maternity policies, they might even have good flexible working policies for working mothers, but how many genuinely apply this equally across the genders.

You see, this world of "Dad" going out to work whilst Mum had a little part time job so she could afford a few new buttons for that dress she was making went out in the 1970's. In the 1980's & 90's the "House Husband" was born, and grew in popularity. Thing is these days both those things are rarer than a fine fillet steak in motorway service area. You see both "mum" & "dad" rightly want their careers to progress equally. The only people that lose out if they don't is the companies themselves who deprive themselves of this potential talent.

Flexibility is more than just allowing someone to work form home occasionally. It needs to be core the values of the business and reflected in everyday practices. These should include:

- Not scheduling meetings early and late
- Provision of appropriate technology to enable remote working
- Clear policies on working remotely that are consistent across all staff grades and departments

Its long been proven that people that if you want something done give it to a busy person. Countless studies have shown that people who work remotely are often more productive (I myself find it much less distracting working in solo environment than in a busy office), and there is little evidence to suggest anything but positive impacts from giving employees this flexibility.

Now of course I appreciate that remote working is not applicable to every role. It's a bit hard to lay bricks if you aren't actually at the building site. But being conscious of the fact that your team, whatever gender they identify as, will probably have commitments outside of work that may require them to have a more flexible hours, can only enhance your employer brand.

Another mistake companies make is when they develop flexible working policies its all about "Mum" or "Dad". What about son with elderly parent, or sister with sibling with extra needs. Companies will often say "well its hard to create a policy that fits all scenarios" – and that's my point. You shouldn't be trying to create a policy that fits every scenario. You should create a set of principles along the lines of, for example:

- "This company supports the principle that employees can work remotely up to 30% of the time"
- or "This company supports the principal that employees can start their working day between 7am-10am"
- Or "No company meeting will start before 10am or after 4pm"

When I have run companies, I have had a very simple approach to employees. You might call it a "Zero Hours Contract", but not the sort that you are thinking of. I always say to my teams, I don't actually care how many hours you sit at your desk for every day, as long as you achieve what we have agreed you will achieve.

Virgin, amongst other successful companies, famously gave every employee unlimited holidays, which actually resulted in employees taking less holidays than when they were given a specific number of days. It comes back to empowering your team, treating them like sentient adults not drones. I think you will find that many of them surprise you.

A word of warning. Flexibility can go to far. I was chatting to a business connection the other day who worked for a Global IT Services firm. Aware he travelled a lot, and worked form home a lot I asked him when he had last been to his office. He said January 2017, when he needed to pick up a new laptop.

Whilst I am a complete evangelist for flexible working, I am even more fervent when it comes to working as a team. I don't care what industry you are in, what role you are in, teamwork always wins. It's very hard to engender team spirit if the team never see each other and no amount of clever technology or video conferencing will ever overcome that hurdle.

If you do operate in a distributed environment with a heavy predominance of working away from other colleagues, you must bring those colleagues together on a regular basis. Personally, I feel a health balance is 1/3 solo and 2/3 team working, but each industry and role is different so I don't feel comfortable being totally prescriptive about that.

Chapter 7 – Using Social Media.

So, this topic scares the living bejeezers out of any business owner, CEO or Executive especially those of a previous generation who really only use facebook to keep tabs on their children's or grandchildren's lives. It's true that social media can be a complete minefield for a company to navigate, but it can also be a very powerful tool.

Now companies have had "intranets" ever since they came out of nappies and became medium sized companies. Big software providers such as Microsoft have done their best to cash in on this with corporate products such as "yammer" which is a bit like Facebook but not as good.

Because these corporate products are "controlled" and "owned" but the company they just aren't powerful enough to impact your employer brand. It's a bit like taking a water pistol to a knife fight. People view these corporate sites with at best suspicion or the worst disdain. One organisation I work with has such a site, and it gets a post ever 4-5 days on average. Now that wouldn't be so bad but the organisation is several thousand people strong and I happen to know their private Facebook pages get about 4-5 posts a minute!

Yes that's right, if you didn't know already, you can have "Private" facebook groups that can only be accessed by employees or people you let join. These groups can be incredibly powerful, because they are already integrated into people's lives, their smartphones & their psyche, they are less reserved, more open and honest. Whilst everyone knows that "management" would be reading this, for some intangible reason (well its probably very tangible to an academic psychologist, which I am not) for some reason they will post and engage more on this sort of group than they will on a corporate intranet group.

Another organisation I work for has dozens of these private pages, pretty much one for every departments, and they are buzzing within information. Sure, there is a odd gripe and groan thread, but also there are dozens of threads of colleagues answering queries from other colleagues on every subject from housing to HR issues.

These ecosystems generate team spirit, they are also very useful bell-weathers for organisational feeling. Here are my rules for setting up these pages:

- Don't set them up, encourage your staff to set them up and moderate them
- By all means post news, information etc (preferably via a team member rather than the CEO or Management posting directly
- Don't get involved in posts! Its going to be very tempting to you to directly answer someone's gripe or comment. Don't do it. Step away from the keyboard. Instead find a way to communicate the correct information to the team as a whole

- Make it clear that the organisation supports the creation and use of these groups, in fact actively encourages it, but also ensure there is a very clear policy in place for social media when it comes to posts that could be offensive or deemed potentially offensive to others.
- Make them reactively moderated. No one is going to post anything apart from positive stuff if their posts don't appear until a moderator "approves" it. I know an organisation that does this, and their Facebook pages are dull as dishwater and about as engaging and atmospheric as a nudist beach in a thunderstorm.

So, don't be frightened of the big bad F. It's free, the technology works, having been beta tested on a few hundred million people, and it's not controllable anyway. At the end of the day if your employees want to set up a "negative" facebook page, they will. I know of several large corporates, including one well known global airline, where the employees have created a very toxic unofficial site. You might as well embrace it and let it have some sort of positive impact on your culture.

By James E. Crawley

Chapter 8 – Communication Communication Communication!

Ok so we have looked at various means of informal communication and ways to engage with your team, but sometimes you just have to tell people what to do. You know all those signs that say "don't grab hold of the cable that's carrying 50,000 volts" etc. I have no problem with this, but there are ways to make these messages more engaging and therefore more noticeable, which after all is surely the point.

Look at these two signs below and think which one had more impact on you and is therefore more effective:

STOP
PLEASE DO NOT FEED THE DUCKS BREAD

Please Don't Feed the Ducks We Have a Special Diet and If We Eat Other Things Like Bread It Can Make Our Tummy's Hurt

Same message, stylistically very different. One is patriarchal, dictatorial and whilst it gets the message across, it almost guarantees a negative reaction. Peoples natural reaction when you say "don't" is to do, just prove the system wrong. With the second example, the message is the same, but it gives the reason in a lighter way. You are more likely to get compliance if you create messages that are engaging to your team.

By James E. Crawley

Chapter 9 – Recruitment

For nearly 20 years, I have operated in and around the talent universe as someone who has hired people, fired people and helped other people literally hire hundreds of others. I think it's fair to say that I have seen the good, the bad and the downright ugly in the field. Don't even for a minute think that global professional service firms or blue-chip companies are a paragon of virtue when compared to struggling start-ups. I have found that organisations – both large and small – have some excellent as well as diabolical processes. Even more shocking is the millions that firms waste on obtaining talent through inefficient process, over-complicated interview schedules and duplication.

Cheaper than recruiting people is retaining people, and retention starts at recruitment. Recruitment is the start of your new employee's journey with you. It sets the initial tone of the relationship, forms their initial impression of you and determines whether they would recommend you as an employer to their peers (potentially the cheapest form of recruitment).

In a public-sector organisation I work with, we do an annual 'Friends and Family'(F&F) test to see if our people would recommend our services to their own families. Employers could do the same thing with their employees. Be warned, as a low F&F test result probably means that you are going to start losing staff if you are not already. It's easier to improve your internal branding with the existing staff.

According to an opinion piece in the marketing website 'The Drum', trust is the key to brand management, and 84% of people trust peer to peer recommendations over any other source of information. So, I will reiterate that retention starts with recruitment, and good recruitment leads to good retention.

We live in a world of first impressions. Brands live, and die, based on these impressions, not only in a B2C sense but more importantly how they are perceived by individuals who could potentially be interested in joining them. We have never been in such an age where impressions of an organisation or company can circulate so quickly around the talent pool. Websites such as vault.com and glassdoor.com even provide potential employees with real reviews from current employees and those who have gone through the interview process. Any employer who doesn't think of themselves as a brand in the talent market and doesn't apply similar principles to how they attract both employees and customers are going to be left behind.

Now I can see what you are thinking. Sure, if we are XYZ Inc., then we need to think about this, but what if we are Google or Microsoft or Amazon. 'I bet we don't have to do this, after all, we will attract 100,000 applications for every role in the company'. My answer is that you have just missed the point. They have *already* done this, which is why they have 100,000 people applying for every role. They are the most attractive employers to work for because they have created such a brand.

One of my favourite quotes, which by the way has been attributed to several key influencers, is 'There are three kinds of people in the world: those who make things happen, those who watch things happen, and those who wonder what happened'. I think it applies to companies as much as it does to individuals. You can place your company in the first category if you want to. It's not about having the hottest product, as what's hot today will be cold tomorrow; it's about having the most alluring proposition for talent. Remember that one person largely developed the original iPod design; James Dyson revolutionised the production of vacuum cleaners, and Richard James, a naval architect, invented the Slinky and made a $250m profit. The right person joining your business could revolutionise it overnight.

You don't need to be Google or Facebook; you just need to create a sustainable brand as a recognised, leading employer in your field. Let's face it. In 10 years, Google or Facebook might not even exist, but even if we go back 30 years, the same principles applied. Growing up, I was interested in hotel management as a career option, and I clearly remember my father saying to me 'Well if you want to go into hotel management, you need to get on the graduate scheme of "Trust House Forte (THF)"'. THF no longer exists, but it was then a shining employer brand – an industry leader and the default destination for a leisure industry graduate in the same way Marks and Spencer (M&S) was for retail. My point is that you don't need to be a cutting-edge technology player or the latest social craze to be an employer brand of choice. You need to be respected as an employer, treat people with respect and be consistent in the way you bring people into the organisation.

One of the most important factors when creating your employer brand is that it must be an honest reflection of your business, ethics and culture. It is pointless attracting someone to your organisation if the second they walk through the door, they are faced with an entirely different reality from the picture you portrayed.

I have a theory about M&S's – steady decline over the past two decades, from "The" High Street brand to "A N Other" . It's my theory, and I have no real evidence to back it up, and I am sure some retail analysts will be able to provide a totally different opinion using pie charts and graphs and probably an app these days. The theory is as follows: M&S used to provide a full range of services to its staff instore from doctors to hairdressers, which made it easy for employees to maintain their health and, more importantly, to return to work. There was a cohort of 'M&S Women' – experienced, returning to work mothers who were only available to join the workforce because of these other services being provided. These experienced women capable of relating to the core M&S customers and also mentor and train younger staff and trainee managers became the company's greatest assets. They were happy to be at work and serve the customers, and the customers were happy to be in the store because of how welcome they felt and the service they got.

Then came along a management consultant who advised M&S that it was much cheaper to let the employees have a sick day to go to the doctor than have a doctor instore. The benefits were withdrawn, and the potential labour pool was, therefore, reduced because M&S was no longer a viable option for busy mothers.

Now the times have changed, and thankfully, working women these days are able to work and deliver excellence in every conceivable role, not just aspire to be an M&S shop assistant, but the same principles still apply. If you look after your workforce, you will gain a reputation for looking after your workforce, and your potential talent pool, therefore, will increase in size.

Daniel Priestley, a business author, has written several well-regarded business programmes. *Oversubscribed*, one of the programmes, is aimed at making companies' sales of products more successful, but if you think about it, it deals with exactly what Facebook or Google are with their talent situation. They have what everyone wants – roles with the organisation that people want to be part of.

Regardless of whether a candidate is successful or not, the recruitment process and how they are treated will impact both their views of the firm and the views of others. It does not take long for feedback to reach the wider market. If the process is poor, the firm could be disregarded by other potential employees.

Kenneth Clarke, not the former Chancellor of the Exchequer but the writer and presenter of the wonderful TV programme *Civilisation*, concluded that the hallmark of a great civilisation is institutionalised courtesy. In this regard, an organisation that has regard for the feelings of others.

Companies that attract and retain staff are those that are progressive, responsive and dynamic, not only in the work that they do but also in the way they recruit. However, front-line operational staff rarely have time to dedicate to a fast and accurate recruitment process, as they are too busy serving customers to devote time for recruitment.

I once spoke to the manager of a mid-sized food supermarket, with about 15 tills and around 30 customer-facing staff on duty. I noticed that only 10 out of the 15 tills were operating, and the rest of the staff were refilling shelves on the shop floor or serving customers at specialist counters, and the lines at the tills were increasing in length. I asked him why he didn't take five staff off replenishing shelves and put them on the tills to reduce the backlog, and he replied, 'It's simple. Those in the queue have already got their products, and it's highly unlikely they will walk away from the trolley they have spent an hour filling just because they have to wait for 5 minutes to check out. Whereas those customers still on the shop floor can only put things in their trolleys in the first place if the products exist on the shelves'. He felt that the best way to serve his customers was to put more emphasis on the 'back office' and replenish the stocks than serve them quickly at the tills.

The same lesson can be applied to talent acquisition. If you constantly are too busy to recruit, then you will never grow because you already are too busy to recruit, and you can only grow through recruitment. It's a vicious circle.

A major misconception is that the shorter the interview process, the higher the chance of hiring the employee. I don't believe this. Over the past few years, we have been asking all our candidates what they are looking for when selecting their next employer. Congenial work and money are at the top of the list, but there are other factors.

- Feeling valued throughout the recruitment process irrespective of whether it leads to a successful appointment or not.
- Being provided accurate information on the company, practice and personalities at all stages of the interview process.
- Being provided specific interview arrangements – pre-planned time and place – and assistance in travel arrangements.
- Being provided fast and accurate feedback on all stages of the interview process.

- Being accorded the opportunity to meet peers in their specific department or practice area.

Only a very small percentage of the candidates were concerned about the time the recruitment process took, the majority of whom were currently unemployed or facing redundancy or uncertainty in their current position.

Whilst the points above may be perceived as 'nannying', the reality of the global talent market is that it is a seller's market for individuals with the requisite skills – after all, a company can only grow by expanding its talent pool. Good candidates have the luxury of picking their employer; therefore, the recruitment process must be extremely professional.

Companies can try to compete financially, but as Tom Clancy, a former Managing Partner of Accenture, once said, 'Money buys only time, not loyalty. A company that competes for talent strictly on cash is vulnerable to the next big offer. This game of escalating salaries is like an arms race – expensive and, ultimately, difficult, if not impossible to win'.

Types of Recruitment

Suppose an employee resigns, or a new position is created. There needs to be some recruitment activity to fill the vacancy. For the sake of argument, assume you are large enough to have someone to look after this (if you don't, then the same principles apply, but you might have to outsource or bring in a specialist interim or contractor). Let's look at the potential options.

- **Internal Recruitment Programmes**

There is quite possibly someone already in the business waiting to step up, maybe a deputy or someone from another part of the business. As a rule, you should always try and promote from within unless you are seeking a brand-new skill set that doesn't exist in your business currently. It does, of course, mean you have to backfill. I have had clients tell me, 'I have the perfect person, and they want this role, but I can't afford to lose them from their current role'. Well, not moving them does not solve the problem; it just means you will probably end up with two roles to fill when your colleague decides that you don't value them, as you didn't give them the role, and leaves.

Why do I say promoting from within is better? First, the candidate knows the organisation, and, therefore, any transition period will be much less painful. They should be able to get a better handover from the existing incumbent if they already have a professional relationship. They will be motivated because you have listened to them and helped progress their career how they wanted it to. Finally, you get the best of both worlds because they still know their old role, which means it's much less risky to hire someone to replace them because they are still around, and if the hiring decision is wrong, you don't have a catastrophic loss of knowledge from your organisation.

So how should you do this internal recruitment? First, if you are in a large organisation, you should advertise the role internally. Just because you have your eye on someone does not mean that they are the only relevant candidate for that role. It also demonstrates to your organisation that you always do your due diligence with decisions that can affect the future of the company.

You should run the same interview process internally as externally (we will come to this later in the book) – the same assessments, interviews, exercises. This is important because of the following:

a) It reaffirms your decision; and

b) It reaffirms to both the employee and their peers that they achieved the role on their merit and capabilities and no other reason. This is especially important in appointing 'Deputies' who step up to the main job.

Obviously, if you are a small company (less than c.20 people), it will probably be clear who the heir apparent should be, but I would still interview the person for the role if nothing to bottom out any concerns they have about stepping up.

- **Ideas for Internal Recruitment Programmes**

You will know already know the candidates in internal recruitment programmes, so it's not always easy to accurately assess them in the same dispassionate way as external candidates. Assuming you only have internal candidates, the following are some suggestions of exercises you could set as a part of the assessment process:

- To design a new company logo reflecting your product and brand values;
- To write a new company strapline/slogan;
- To prepare a one-page executive summary of a briefing document; and
- To design a new product or service for the company.

- **External Peer-Peer/Employee Referral Programmes**

I have deliberately split external recruitment into a few categories. Earlier we learnt that 84% of people rely on peer to peer information than any other source. In other words, if you have 10 people in your company, you potentially have 10 marketers who can help your source talent. Peer to peer referrals is the gold standard of recruitment programmes.

If you have a strong employee referral programme, then the majority of your recruitments should be done for you. If you are being recommended by your employees to their peers and connections, then you know you have a good employer brand. If this is the situation for your organisation, then put this book down, go, celebrate and come back to this book when the situation changes.

There are a variety of ways to motivate your team to refer vacancies to their networks, and some examples are as follows:

- **Money** – A financial reward, maybe a percentage of what you would pay an external provider, is a strong incentive; however, it should not be the primary motivator. If you have to rely on hard currency, then you probably haven't built a strong enough employer brand yet, so you might want to revisit that first.
- **Social rewards** – Hard-to-find concert tickets, an amazing meal at a top restaurant or maybe something substantial such as an engraved watch are relevant options. If you gave someone a £5,000 watch rather than £5,000 in cash, every time they look at the watch, probably for years ahead, they will think of your company in a positive light.
- **Team incentives** – If you have departments in your organisation, you could have a competition about how many employee referrals they can achieve in a quarter with some sort of team away day for the highest performing team.
- **Charitable donations** – A charitable donation to a cause selected by the referrer is another option. With this, you also

have the added benefit to include this in your Corporate Social Responsibility Programme.

What I will say is that if you haven't followed similar principles to those outlined in Sandy Asch's book, then you are unlikely to have a strong enough brand to be able to rely on this channel.

External Recruitment – Outside Sources
External recruitment seems simple but, in fact, is highly complex and where most firms waste money and make mistakes.

There are two ways to do it – you can either do it yourself or with a third-party provider. Then within the latter, there are various methodologies you can use – Executive Search, Contingent Agency Recruitment, Advertised Selection. We need to break this down a bit and highlight the benefits and challenges or risks of both.

There is a growing trend for firms to try and 'in-source' their recruitment and rely less on external agencies. Frankly, I applaud this. Why you ask. Well, in my view, many external providers charge far too much to recycle a CV from LinkedIn, and those firms leave the client wondering exactly where the added value is. It is, therefore, completely right that the client should seek to build their own function to source great talent from this cost-effective source. In fact, JCM trains client teams to do exactly this. There are, however, limits to this activity, and the clients who think that having built this team now give an 'in-house executive search capability' are often sadly mistaken.

Using a Provider
First, you have to select your recruitment partner(s), but all recruitment firms can look the same to an inexpert eye. They are not. Forget about the glossy websites, the talks of hundreds of professionals they have in their global practices, the amazing database of talent they have and ask the following two questions:
- Tell me about the last five similar positions you have recruited for; and
- Introduce me to the exact team who will be working on this project.

Don't worry about terms and conditions and fee rates at this stage, as they are all negotiable and will all fall into the same sort of brackets eventually. You need to be confident that you are not being sold 'the Partner' and then being served by 'the Associate' and they understand your business and, more importantly, your business culture.

Once you have selected your external firm, then go through the terms and conditions because there can be significant differences.

Expenses: Some firms will try and charge you expenses on top of their professional fees. I am not talking about large expenses, such as those of airline tickets to go and interview candidates, but a fixed % of the fee to cover 'administration'. This is an archaic practice, generally enforced by the larger traditional firms, and it's nonsense. It's purely a mechanism to increase profit margins, and I have seen some firms charge up to 8% of the total fee. JCM doesn't charge its clients any expenses except exceptional expenses, such as travel, and any such sums are agreed in advance, itemised and recharged a cost

Stage payments: There is no problem with paying the fee in stages, and most quality firms will insist on an initial fee or retainer. We generally charge 1/3rd of our fees on the commencement of the project because it can take months until the next stage, and like any business, we have to ensure cash flow. However, once the first instalment is paid, the subsequent payments should be based on the deliverables. You should have a report or a shortlist or whatever stage you agree. Too many firms still try to charge stage payments on a time basis. I came across a client a few years ago who had paid out nearly £200k in stage payments and was yet to interview a single candidate.

Guarantees: Any search firm or agency confident in its ability will have absolutely no problem in guaranteeing an appointment for three months, and the better firms will guarantee for six months. This gives you the certainty that if the appointment doesn't work out because the candidate is not the right person for the role, then the firm will re-run the recruitment exercise at no additional costs to you.

The selection of the external needs is to be done by you and your colleagues, not led by a procurement department. I have responded to dozens of procurement requests in my career, and they all use the same stock questions around our policies, diversity targets, among others. Not one of them has ever effectively asked me to demonstrate our capability to understand our client's business or actually deliver the mandates that are going to be required.

JCM runs assessment panels for clients selecting recruitment partners, and we use interview-based techniques as if we are hiring a candidate. Once we have made our shortlist, we check functional items, such as the presence of indemnity insurance, diversity policies, to name a few.

If you do this properly, you can build a partnership with your external provider. Note that I am not using the word 'supplier' here. You don't want a supplier. A supplier is for stationary or furniture or printer toner cartridges. Suppliers sell you commodities and send you a box of Quality Street at Christmas. When you are talking about talent, you don't want to be sold to, and you don't want a commodity.

A true partnership model will build a relationship between you and your external consultant to the point that they emotionally invest in your business and your journey. This is where the magic happens, and this is where you start saving. If you trust your recruitment partner, you don't need to spend time reading stacks of CVs; you can just accept that the candidates presented are competent and have them booked into your diary. If you trust your recruitment partner's knowledge of your business, you don't need to spend much time briefing every time a role comes up. If you don't think that your recruitment partner is trying to sell to you, you can use their wise counsel when making the tough decision between two excellent candidates.

In the best recruitment processes I have been a part of and witnessed, the recruitment partner's job does not end when the shortlist is done. They have sat in the room or even taken an active part in the interview process, then guided the discussions amongst the key stakeholders after the interviews. My clients and I have often joked that they need to print me a security pass and find me a desk as I am in the building so often during a recruitment campaign.

I could write a whole book on supplier selection (maybe the difficult second book), but let me sum it up for you here in some key points:
- Know what you are committing to and what they are committing to;
- Make sure you both have a clear understanding who is doing what in the process;
- Make sure the rewards are tied to deliverables; and
- Remember, this consultant is going to represent your brand in the marketplace. Do they exude your brand values?

Methods Of Recruitment

As we have already discussed, there are several methods of recruitment, utilising different mediums, some of which are more suited to a particular set of requirements than others.

Head Hunting or Executive Search (to give it its more respectable title)
Head-hunting is probably the most accurate way to identify suitable candidates for an organisation. This does not, however, mean it is a suitable solution for all situations. Headhunting is time-consuming but can produce optimum results against a specific brief. It is certainly not always the most cost-effective solution for hiring junior to middle management personnel, and we would generally recommend it only for individual senior appointments that cannot be sourced elsewhere and for highly sensitive positions.

Many clients ask me why they can't do this themselves. Simply put, whether this activity is done internally or externally, remember that sourcing/identifying candidates is only 30% of the process. Some firms and most internal teams rely purely on web resources such as LinkedIn, which is indeed a powerful tool for identifying and approaching candidates. Last time I checked, however, it was inadequate at keeping candidates motivated throughout a six-month recruitment process, and it's terrible at negotiations. You cannot replace an experienced talent consultant with a database however strong its CRM functions are.

Executive search is not about finding the talent. Anyone with an internet connection can do it these days. It's about a comprehensive candidate assessment and benchmarking exercise. It's a candidate care exercise, keeping the shortlist motivated during a 3-, 6-, 12-month selection process. It's about providing insight and knowledge on the market for the duration of the search, not pushing the first candidate past the finishing post. It's about advising the client when they are wrong and suggesting constructive ways forward.

The reason clients should be paying the extra % for an executive search is simple – they are paying for years of experience, years of lessons learnt. Too many times I see clients repurpose HR professionals into recruiters and expect them to provide a similar service as an experienced search professional. That's like asking a bus driver to take a spin in Lewis Hamilton's Mercedes and win the Monaco Grand Prix.

If companies truly want an executive search function, then build an executive search function. That involves hiring experienced search professionals to lead it, not re-tasking HR or internal recruitment managers. A few firms have done this over the years, and it has paid massive dividends. PA Consulting set up a Partner Recruitment Acquisition team back in the 1990s, staffed by experienced executive search personnel and led by Roselyn Cason-Marcus, my good friend, who now leads Partner Acquisition for McKinsey &Co. Over the years, they saved literally millions of pounds on executive search fees because they used external providers for less than 10 % of their open partner positions.

Other firms have tried on a more basic budget, and whilst I wouldn't say they have failed, they certainly haven't fulfilled their potential.

For years people have asked me if I am worried about the impact of the internet with sites such as LinkedIn on my business. My answer is no because they are not taking the market share of my business. They have taken market share from the low-end contingent market, and rightly so, as why should a client pay 20-25% for a CV from an active job seeker that's readily available online? We would encourage, support and train our clients' teams to reduce their spending on that channel.

Clients also ask me whether technology will replace the need for executive search. More and more articles are appearing about the great work that IBM's Watson, among others, is doing in the field of recruitment and how soon executive search will be obsolete. Sorry Skynet, but we have had this prediction before, with the internet in general, then Monster, then LinkedIn. If anything, technology seems to provide a growthspurt to the numbers of recruiters, not a reduction.

Now don't get me wrong – I am a technologist, and I believe technology plays an essential role in the talent management lifecycle. Technology helps the human element avoid mistakes; it securely collates and distributes data; it schedules accurately and provides analytical data at the end of the campaign. It enhances rather than degrade the humanist aspects of the process.

Technology cannot totally replace the human input because we are dealing with humans. These days finding candidates and analysing their CVs into a long list probably only accounts for 10% of the role. The human process management, the cultural fit assessment (more important than ever before to both candidates and companies these days) and the hand holding through the process are roles a machine cannot take on in the foreseeable future. I bet even Google doesn't have an algorithm to measure 'Googliness' (1/4 of their selection criteria).

Would you want to work for a company that selects you purely by a computer algorithm?

The issue with any system is that it is generally designed by engineers. The issue with most recruitment systems seems to be that they are designed by engineers and HR personnel, and unfortunately, HR is a different discipline from recruitment.

Don't get me wrong. I applaud the amazing work these engineers and machines are doing, but don't write off humanity yet.

Advertised Selection Campaigns
Companies' greatest problem in times of growth is often the lack of quality candidates who are physically coming through the door. Many smaller firms have the added problem that they do not currently command a high profile amongst candidates in the marketplace. Therefore, a solution to this for growing companies is to use some sort of advertising to boost their candidate throughput. Whilst advertisements can draw huge numbers of inappropriate candidates, generally good ones can result in one or two placements. The number of responses only becomes a factor when you do not have the back-office machinery in place to handle the process. By

allowing for an element of advertising, you achieve three things. First, raising the company's profile amongst candidates and potential clients. Second, a greater throughput of candidates. Third, potential cost saving on agency and outside supplier's fees, if you run the process in-house. Selection is a very powerful tool when used well.

Historically, senior appointments were featured in broadsheet newspapers' appointment sections or on specific websites. Junior or technical roles were featured in specialist trade press or on high volume technology sites (and still are). I used to work for a company that made almost as much money out of selling job advertisements to the Sunday Times as they did actually placing people. These days clients have many more tools at their disposal.

Specialist online recruitment sites still heavily feature executive appointments; however, I would hypothesise that actually more senior recruitment is conducted on broader content sites, such as LinkedIn, than any other medium currently.

LinkedIn has a range of tools, many of which are aimed at the corporate in-house recruiter, and frankly, if your company and your role are attractive, all you should need is a good in-house recruiter to sift through the CVs and make the interview arrangements. If the cost of a LinkedIn advertisement is £500, then why wouldn't you try this channel first and save yourself £40k–100k of recruitment fees?

Many leading search firms will tell you that 'No one really good or senior will apply for a job on LinkedIn', and that may be true, but Bob might see the advertisement for a Senior VP of finance and just pick up the phone to call his former colleague Pam, who happens to be your current CFO and is running the advertisement. Just because someone doesn't reply to a specific email address doesn't mean that they haven't arrived via that channel.

My first question to a new executive search client is 'What have you done so far to source someone for this role'? If it's not a particularly sensitive role, and they haven't explored options such as LinkedIn, I will suggest that they do before they engage me. Why? Because there is nothing worse than being three days into a project, with a third of our fees paid, and then someone hearing about the role and contacting their old pal directly. Whilst technically we are fully entitled to our fee and probably a cancellation fee as well, it doesn't leave a nice taste in the mouth.

I have never charged a cancellation fee from a client in such a situation, and often, if we really haven't spent much time on a project, we will also give them some credit towards their next assignment on the basis that we are partners in their enterprise and the long-term client relationship is more important to us than any short-term gain.

This is not to be confused with clients who brief us, then continue to brief other firms and run their own campaign. We demand exclusivity on a project, not for financial reasons, but for the simple fact that if one person doesn't have control of the project, its likely to tip itself up and crash and burn.

Contingency Agency Recruitment
People in "blue-blooded" search firms tend to look down on contingency agencies with a mixture of pity and condescension. I have operated at the highest levels of the blue-blooded search arena and the highly commoditised contingency arena and have been successful in both. There is no qualitative difference between really

good search firms and really good contingent firms. They are both capable of excellent work, but their function and methodologies are very different.

It's like comparing a shrimp fisherman, who uses a net, with a lobster fisherman, who uses a pot. Neither is better or worse; it just depends on what you want to catch as to how you go about it.

No recruitment company can claim to have total coverage of the marketplace in terms of the available active candidates, and so in order to secure your market share of CVs, you sometimes need to cast a wide net over as many agencies as practicable. Limiting yourself by too small of a preferred supplier list can cut a huge number of smaller independent firms out of the supply chain. As a result, you can potentially miss out on a large number of candidates.

Many companies find themselves overwhelmed by the number of random CVs they receive from agencies, and many of these are little more than rebadged LinkedIn profiles sent out on mailshots. I have received three CVs for technical developers this week from an agency, all of them for technical developers. I have never employed and can't ever see myself employing a technical developer. This can be avoided by a slick and effective process, in which outside suppliers only supply to requests. If you get the process right, then the number of agencies receiving those requests and sending you content becomes less relevant.

Contingency recruitment is a powerful tool that has both benefits and risks. Generally, higher volume campaigns for a large number of similarly skilled individuals lend themselves to contingency recruitment, but equally low volume campaigns seeking senior talent on a reactive basis can lend themselves to contingency methods. If you don't have a burning platform or a specific date when you must appoint someone, then maybe a passive contingency campaign to see what's available on the market is suitable.

Pros
- Casts a wide net over the talent pool; and
- No direct costs (we will revisit this later in the book) involved unless you hire someone.

Cons
- You don't get exclusivity on the candidates; and
- It's hard to build a partnership with your supplier.

Graduate/MBA Milk round

Many companies make the mistake of treating the recruitment of graduates from top universities as similar to normal recruitment. Graduates from top universities and business schools have a wealth of information and opportunities supplied to them. They can pick and choose their next company. In order to address this area, companies must have a unique offering that attracts graduates and MBAs. The first approach must be to target the university staff, add value to their offerings by making personnel available for talks and lectures, sponsor events and provide resources. The second approach must be directed at the students, by providing literature and digital content initially, followed up by visits by both senior and junior personnel with similar backgrounds on special recruitment days. Also, providing graduate placement schemes for vacation periods, sponsorship of studies, fun-days and, also, opportunities for MBA students to work on projects alongside existing teams can be beneficial.

Specialist Programmes

It is not uncommon these days for companies to have the need for a specialist recruitment programme. This could be because they need people with very specific new technology skills or, more commonly, have an issue with something like diversity. In fact, this is so common now that Sandra Guzman and Nathalie Mawdsley, my good friends and colleagues, left the mainstream executive search world to establish a specialist diversity consultancy – Unida Consulting. They assist clients with this very issue from both thought leadership and practical perspective. I would strongly recommend anyone interested in this topic to check out some of their excellent content at http://www.unidaconsulting.com/

If your company finds itself in such a situation, then my strongest recommendation is to bring in the experts, whoever they may be. Trying to fix the situation yourself is likely to fail, considering that the shortfall developed under your watch in the first place. Remember that everything we are trying to do here is to build your employer brand. If you launch a new product, you will advertise it – you need to be thinking along the same lines here.

Foreign Hire Programmes

People sometimes forget that there are some amazing talent pools elsewhere of both foreign talent but also potential returnee talent. The economic conditions in one geographic area might have prompted talent to shift abroad, but maybe it's time for that talent to come back. Your challenge, which really is stating the obvious, is logistics. You need to think about this in the following three areas:
- How are you going to interview?

- How are you going to relocate the successful candidates?
- How are you going to treat people who may have to return if visa rules change?

I would strongly advise involving a specialist partner who can utilise the resources of the local market that you are trying to target. Every situation will be different, and you may have to grapple with the complexity of mapping international qualifications and professional registrations.

Think this strategy through very carefully. In my experience, this can provide a relatively quick short-term fix; however, this migratory talent pool is likely to move onto the next favourable geographical area as the economic cycle progresses.

Chapter 9 ¾ – The True Costs of Recruitment

Ask someone how much it costs to recruit an employee, and they would probably say that 'It cost us x £s for the advertisement', or 'We had to pay an agency 23%'. The actual answer is slightly more complex because people generally forget about their and their own staff time involved in the process.

A more accurate cost, therefore, is as follows:

(a) The cost of the recruitment medium + (b) The cost of the employers own staff time

Now how many of you actually know what you cost? I am not talking about the cost of employing you, your wages, insurance but the cost of you doing a task for a business. For a salesperson, this is relatively easy to work out. There are approximately 260 working days in a calendar year, take out 10% for holidays, sickness, training, among others, and you are left with approximately 234 working days. If a salesman's target is £1m a year, then their daily cost is as follows:

$$£1,000,000 / 234 = £4,473$$

Therefore. The hourly cost of this individual conducting interviews rather than selling your product is £534

For individuals who don't hold such a target, it should still be possible to work out what their value is to the business is each year (if you can't, then you probably don't need them) and subsequently, a daily and hourly rate.

This exercise is very valuable, and I would encourage companies to do it for all their employees. It's one of the most powerful metrics available to you in business, as you can instantly understand the cost of an away day, holding a weekly meeting, running a special internal project, but we are digressing; let's get back to talent!

Now having established the base cost, we need to count in additional factors such as the following:
- The cost of having an interim whilst the role is vacant;
- The cost on the productivity of having the role vacant; and
- The additional load that affects the other employees of having the role vacant.

All the above need to be multiplied by the number of days until the new employee joins.

I would hazard an educated guess that on an average the true cost of recruiting someone, especially a replacement of someone, is at least **140-150%** of their first year's actual cost.

It's rather important then that this be sorted. You do it efficiently; you do it professionally, and make your process stand out amongst your competitors.

Duplication

Another hidden cost of recruitment is duplication. It really occurs only in larger firms who are looking for similar profiles across multiple geographies. But when it does happen, it is rife! I once came across an instance of one of the world's top 4 professional services firms who was running the same search out of 8 different geographic locations.

Concerning a middle management role these days, you have to consider your talent pool to be at least regional if not global. The organisation mentioned above had a regional structure in place, but local hiring even at the £500k + level was done locally. Five different executive search firms (yes, some firms were retained more than once) had been mandated with retainers of c.£25,000 and were all searching for the same profile of the individual. When we looked deeper into the process, we found there was over a 30% overlap of shortlisted candidates across the five shortlists. Irrespective of who got hired, the firm was going to be paying five firms for either completing or cancelling the searches.

The fact that there was no co-ordination meant that the firm was going to waste nearly £400,000 just on a single recruitment. When we analysed their overall £50m annual spending, we identified savings of nearly £10m within a few hours of looking at the data by eliminating duplication.

By James E. Crawley

Chapter 10 – The Recruitment Process

So, what does good look like? Fast is not necessarily good; neither is cheap nor expensive. Good is efficient; good treats people with respect and the way you would want to be treated. Whether you are hiring a CEO or a security guard, the basic principles remain the same.

Every business has a process. Julian Thomas and Andrew Williams of Maisha & Co, my good friends and both ex-senior partners of Big 4 consulting firms, can talk to you about the process for weeks on end. I am no expert, but what I have learnt in the past twenty odd years is that if there is a good process, then the outcome is immeasurably more likely to be positive than if you make it up as you go.

I have refined my recruitment process down to basically five distinct stages. I will gladly challenge anyone who says that you need more than this. I have placed very senior £1m+ individuals in five stages or less, and I have also experienced the 27-stage process for the same level of individual. The only difference – one started 12 months sooner and had already made his organisation £10m by the time other candidate had agreed on a start date.

I think its fear that makes people add stages – fear that they will be the one making the decision, fear that if it's the wrong decision, then they are going to suffer. If that's truly the culture of your organisation, then you have bigger problems than recruitment.

My plea to hiring managers, therefore, is to please be bold. You will make mistakes. It happens, get over it, because the paralysis of not hiring someone and waiting for all your colleagues to agree is killing the growth of your company.

Do you think Mark Zuckerberg, Larry Ellison or Richard Branson put their potential executive hires through 27 rounds of interviews? Of course, they don't.

The other important part of the process, before we get down to the detail, is your employer brand. See, that's cropped up again strangely enough. Now I know that you are a very important and busy person, with lots of client commitments and very important meetings to attend. That does not give you the right to stand a candidate up or cancel a meeting with them half an hour before its due to start. That's not you being an important busy person; that's you being a schmuck (I would have used a strong word here, but my publisher wouldn't let me). You have no idea what your candidate has had to do to make their diary work for this meeting. They too might have important client commitments or important meetings. They also have the added disadvantage of having to 'disappear' from their current employment to talk to you, a competitor. What are they supposed to say when their Boss finds them at their desk and says, 'Emily I thought you were at the dentist this afternoon?' 'Oh yes, Sarah, he cancelled because he was busy?'

I have had clients who have stood people up, without reason, three times. No pre-warning, they just either don't dial into the call or don't show up for the meeting. It's rude; it's inconsiderate, and more importantly, it tarnishes your 'Employer Brand'. So, at the end of the week, when Emily is at Corny & Barrow with her two friends, recounting the week's events and being asked about her interview at ZZZ consulting, and she tells her two eminently qualified friends that she was stood up for the meeting, you have probably just lost two more people from your potential talent pool. But you haven't just lost two people because they might tell their friends about how arrogant the management at ZZZ is, and one of those people will probably blog about it on glassdoor.com or vault.com.

When you drop even the tiniest stone into a still pond of water, it never enters without a ripple.

Whenever I do executive search these days, I follow a rule. Two strikes, and you're out. What I mean by this is if the candidate is stood up two times throughout the interview process, then I will recommend to the candidate to withdraw from the process because this client clearly does not respect them. More importantly I will tell the client I am doing it as well!

Now, life happens; things in diaries move; mistakes are made, but they don't have to be an issue. My 'respect' test happens when the client rings me and says, 'I can't make it, or I was stuck in a meeting, but I would like to ring the candidate myself and explain that and make a new arrangement.' When that happens, I know its genuine. I respect the client, but more importantly, the candidate respects the client.

We are going to move on now to some more specific bits of advice around the process. If you are a CEO or not the individual who actually runs the recruitment process, then feel free to skip this bit and come back later when your recruiter comes back with a plan, so you can see what good looks like.

Planning

Most recruitment practices follow the same basic principle and happen in the following four main stages:
- Identification of need and production of material;
- Decision of recruitment methods;
- Actual recruitment process; and
- Feedback evaluation and review.

Identification of Need and Production of Material

If you are replacing an employee, identification of need is simple – we have lost an HR director; therefore, we need an HR director. However, it's always good practice when a vacancy occurs to ask the question 'Do we still need an X in that role'? Sometimes companies evolve and grow tremendously since the initial role was created, and the absence of someone gives an ideal opportunity to review the current shape of the organisation.

When I am working with clients, the easiest way I follow to establish the level of need is to find out how easy it is for someone to write a job description for the role that is not a generic 'HR Director' job description copied from the internet, but a tailored document concerning the individual organisation and challenges to be faced.

Production of Job Descriptions and Person Specification

Whilst each hire is individual, many similar skilled candidates may be hired in a year in some situations. In order to minimise repeated work and speed up the process, draft job descriptions and person specifications should be pre-written. This will mean that only a small amount of time to update the basic specification will be required in order to fit it into a particular role.

Even if this is not the case, every key person in the organisation should be asked to write their job description. It's a useful exercise and can be used to build career development plans for your staff. We often find with clients who have grown quickly that formal job descriptions have never existed, so I would strongly encourage this situation be rectified sooner rather than later, and who better to write a job description than the person currently doing the job!

The core of job descriptions and person specifications should be standard for your organisation and contain similar base information so that they are familiar to the staff and managers who provide the core material for their detail.

They should contain as much information as possible; however, as a minimum, the following must be included:

Job Description	**Person Specification**
Job Title	Personal Attributes
Company Description / Overview of the Opportunity	Qualifications or Experience
	Special Clearances (Security)
Line responsibilities	Specialist Knowledge
External responsibilities	Mobility
Salary and Remuneration	
Location	

Chapter 11 – References

Why take references? It's a simple enough question. Why are you taking references? Are you unsure as to the robustness of your own interview process? Do you doubt your colleagues' ability to assess a candidate so much that you think asking the candidates to give you the names of three people who really like them is going to be a game changer? Seriously, who in their right mind is going to give you the names of three people who are going to say anything that isn't glowing about them? These '360' references have been dreamed up in the cauldron of HR and serve no purpose other than to tick a box saying, 'Yes Boss, I have taken up references'.

I am not talking about qualification checks, visa checks, criminal record checks, among others, but about the three people listed at the bottom of the CV as 'references available on request'.

I was once offered a job I didn't want with a large company; the money was great, the role sounded significant, but I just didn't feel a connection throughout the interview process with a number of key stakeholders. They were really keen and nice people, but I struggled to articulate how to say no to the role. Then I thought, 'Simple; they won't hire me if my references are bad'. I couldn't possibly ask any of my friends or colleagues or clients to give me a bad reference, so I hatched a plan and created three people (I also wanted to test my theory on references). They were as follows:

- Bobby Jones – My 'Director' at a previous company;
- Zak Orfman – A previous client; and
- Tony Woolgar – A consultant who used to work for me.

With the wonders of Gmail, Hotmail and Skype, they all had a phone number and email address, and sure enough, each of them was contacted by the head-hunter (yes, even head-hunters use head-hunters).

Bear in mind that the person who made the calls was the same person who had first contacted me about the role, interviewed me, spoke to me after every meeting with feedback (Yes, I know what you are thinking – this head-hunter gives excellent service) and must have had spoken to me at least thirty times in the span of three weeks, and the person at the other end of the phone was me. I had done my best to alter my voice slightly, but let me tell you, John Culshaw and Rory Bremner have nothing to fear from me. Each call had lasted around ten minutes and covered the same questions as supplied to the head-hunter by the client:

The questions were as follows: 'What are James' strengths?' 'What are James' weaknesses?' 'Name a challenging situation James dealt with that you have personal knowledge?' 'Would you employ/work with / work for (delete as appropriate) James again?' 'Is there anything else we haven't covered that we should know?' – my absolute favourite.

Of course, the mischievous side of me couldn't help myself. Bobby was very enthusiastic about James and very keen that he got the role because it took James out of the competitive area that he was in. However, when asked about weaknesses, he did go on for about 5 minutes about various character flaws. Zak was very quiet, almost monosyllabic and clearly uncomfortable about giving a reference because his employer forbade him from giving references. The call with Tony was fine until we reached the 'name a challenging situation' question where he went to on describe how James had managed to help his MD escape from the police out of the toilet window following a punch-up at company sales conference.

So, all in all, they were not the most glowing of references. Every time one of the referees put up a negative, such as compulsive obsessive behaviour, the head-hunter would try and turn it into a positive, such as 'Ah, so is it fair to say he is obsessed with accuracy and detail then'?

It made not a lot of difference, and I don't know to this day whether the references actually even made it to the client or not. My point, therefore, is that it is a pointless exercise. Now there are going to be some people in my industry spitting their dummies out right about now because they make a good living off of taking references; in fact, some firms even charge extra for it above and beyond their normal fees.

Let me provide a little insider tip right now that would get me kicked out of the magic circle if there was such a thing for headhunters. We love taking references. 'Why?' I hear you ask. Because it provides at least three free business development leads. We get to speak to someone for as long as we like, and we can start building rapport with a potential captive lead while taking the reference. When I worked in a large PLC search environment, if you didn't come away from referencing with a new client meeting, you were considered to have failed. It was the raison d'etre of the whole exercise.

If the candidate has provided the references, then discard them. True 360-degree referencing can be done by higher quality search firms. When I take a reference, I ask the candidate for the three people they suggest, and sure enough, I take those three references (Well I don't want to miss out on a good business development opportunity, do I?), but then the process changes. I then search those three individuals' networks to identify other individuals that I am connected to and that are likely to have known the candidate, and I will keep doing this until I have found enough references to back up and check information that has come out of the interview process. I won't provide names to my client and identify who said what, but I will collate this information and present a summary.

Quality referencing, properly done, can add value to the decision-making process, and it is the reason, I believe, for my proudest statistic from my time as a recruitment professional. It's not the hundreds of searches I have completed, but that no one I placed ever left within the twelve-month guarantee period I always offered my clients.

Chapter 12 – Other Tools and Their Value in Creating your Employer Brand

Every generation of employee looks for different things from their employers, regardless of whether it is the Baby Boomers, Generation X, Y, Millennials (the Avocado generation). Suppose, for argument sake, that you have read, agreed with and implemented every nugget of wisdom in this book, and you now have a world-class, awesome recruitment process that you can be proud of. You know that any potential employee is going to be impressed by your challenging interview questions, comprehensive feedback loops, candidate information, among others. The only problem is that next door to your shiny futuristic HQ building is an almost identical building housing a direct competitor who has also read this book (I believe other books are available, but I can't attest to their quality!).

What next? How else do you make your employer brand stand out? Well, recruitment done well is a process. Employment, however, needs to contain a much wider variety of softer attributes. The good news is that these attributes are tangible; the bad news is they are all hard to implement. Let's tick some of them off, one by one.

Diversity

As I already might have mentioned, I have some friends who can help you with this. Irrespective of your industry, quality potential employees want to work for organisations with no institutional bias around nationality, gender, sexuality, disability and that contain a diverse talent pool. Sure, you might be in a traditional industry that has a historical problem with some of these, but that, in itself, is not the problem. What you are doing about it is the problem and is reflected in the attraction for someone to join.

I once had a client (well, not a client because we didn't accept the work) who approached us and asked us to provide them with some women-only shortlists. I asked them why, and they answered that they had an issue because they had no senior executives who were female. Fair enough, and had they stopped there, I probably would have signed them as a client, but they then went on and blew their foot off with a cruise missile by saying, 'We are going for a public listing on AIM, and we have to be seen to be doing the right thing'. Wrong answer. The sentence alone summed up for me their real attitude to female talent and the corrosive and unhealthy environment that boardroom would be for any female executive to sit in.

If you have an issue, be honest about it, and be honest to candidates about what you are planning or, even better, are actually doing about it.

Corporate Social Responsibility

What self-respecting company these days doesn't have a CSR agenda? The fact you have one is not going to be enough. It has to resonate with both your employees and your customers, and it needs to be meaningful. There is a whole chapter on this in the book, heave a read, its good even if I do say so myself.

Eco-Credentials

'Do you use green energy?' 'Are your buildings efficient?' 'Do you recycle?' 'How is your carbon footprint?' 'Do you have a bike or car share scheme?' 'Do you have electric charging points for vehicles in your car park?' These matter to many individuals. Whilst to many people, these are not important considerations, but to enough people, they are. I can think of several candidates I have had on shortlists who have turned down roles because of a company's environmental policies.

Flexibility

Again I have written a whole chapter about this so I won't repeat myself.

Ethics

Depending on the industry, it can be easy to highlight your ethical stance in some situations but harder in others. If you are a bank like Unity that has strict rules as to what type of companies can open accounts with you or an importer of manufactured goods that will only deal with suppliers that meet certain standards of employment conditions in their factory, then you should be able to shout about your ethical practices from the rooftops. If, however, you run a large gambling website, then however 'ethical' you make your product sound, you will remain the devil incarnate to some people. So, what am I saying here? Be honest, be open and be true to whatever you are. Don't try and present yourself as something you are not. In the internet age, any candidate can quickly suss out what is and what isn't the truth.

Fun

Is it fun to work at your company? Does it provide stimulation in addition to what's in your wallet? Do you provide facilities such as onsite or nearby gyms and catering? Do you want to know why successful companies put subsidised coffee franchises in their lobbies? It is not because they like their employees and want to give them cheap coffee; instead they want to keep their employees inside the building so that the employees are around more and end up being more productive for the company.

Google takes it one step further and provides completely free food and drinks at their main campus so that the employees are around from breakfast to dinner. There is a famous story about Brandon, a 23-year-old Google employee from Massachusetts, who actually lives in a truck in the Google car park and saves 90% of his income because he has no living costs. Living on site, every conceivable facility is provided to him from Doctors to Zumba classes.

I am not suggesting that you encourage such behaviour but think about the facilities you provide your employees. If all you have is a chocolate vending machine in your lobby and you work in the middle of an industrial estate, I would suggest you take a good hard look at how you are looking after your people. Simple things, such as decent showers and bike parking for all those who wish to cycle to work, arranging taster sessions for yoga and alternative therapies during lunch breaks, bringing in interesting speakers for seminars, don't have to cost the earth but can have an earth shattering impact on your employer brand.

None of this should even be a surprise to you, as I am not coming down the mountain with carved stone tablets. However, as with most things in life, it's the obvious things we forget.

Pay
I am not going to spend much time on pay, as frankly, it really doesn't affect your employer brand unless you are paying more than 10% differential to the market.

Pay your employees what you yourself would like to be paid for the role they are doing. A good company can split its earnings into 3 pots: 1/3rd for the shareholders, 1/3rd for the staff and 1/3 to invest in the growth of the company.

If you apply the same principle to your employees, they should generally be rewarded with 1/3rd of what they bring to the company, be that in sales and revenue, products or processes.

Personally, I have never had a salary negotiation for myself during the recruitment process. When asked about pay by a potential employer, I have always answered, 'Pay me what you think I am worth', and I have never been disappointed.

If you apply these principles, you won't go far wrong.

The Zany, Wacky and Ridiculous

Now it might come as some surprise to you that I am not a fan of the "wacky races" recruitment practices. If you care to go on Google, or any of your favourite search engines, and type in 'Wacky Recruitment Ideas', you will get pages of listings. What you will notice when reading those, after you have recovered from your sense of disappointment, is that none of them are actually that wacky. I know I was disappointed that not one of the suggestions included a hot air balloon, a lawn mower or a karaoke rendition of Pink!'s latest album.

Why? Because wacky really doesn't work. We are not recruiting clowns for the circus (apologies if you are the HR director for Cirque du Soleil – this probably isn't the book for you); we are recruiting professionals. My exception to this rule is first-time graduates. Do what you like with graduates because a) they love a challenge, and b) anything you have concocted, they have seen coming from a mile away anyway.

By all means, be creative. Not every interview has to be two people looking at each other across a desk, but getting a candidate to do the interview in Morse code by tapping on the wall opposite probably is taking it too far

Chapter 13 – Your HR Department Is Not Your Recruitment Department

One of the big mistakes that companies of all sizes make is misusing their HR department and thinking that they are qualified to lead recruitment activities for the organisation.

Now don't get me wrong. I am not devaluing the role of the HR team here at all; I am doing quite the opposite, in fact. HR teams add significant value to any organisation; however, just because recruitment is about people, it doesn't mean it's about HR per se. It's similar, I guess, to the differential between your sales department and your marketing department. Both departments are about getting your product into the market, but both, whilst connected, have different functions.

Of course, many HR personnel have recruitment experience but think about what we are trying to achieve here throughout this book – enhancing your employer brand.

When you order a club sandwich at 2am from a Michelin star restaurant in a five-star hotel, is it the chef who runs the restaurant or a special night chef employed for that task who makes it for you?

Both are chefs; both make delicious food, but one is a specialist in one area, and the other is a specialist in another area.

If you want to be the leading employer brand in the marketplace, then the night chef isn't going to cut it – you need the expert, the true specialist who is going to set you apart from every other firm out there.

You are trying to build a following, and people follow what is new or unique or where they perceive the existence of added value.

Now, for a lot of companies, having a full-time recruitment professional sitting around to do occasional appointments would be very wasteful. There, however, are options. An option is to rely on an external recruitment consultancy or search firm. Remember, earlier we spoke about the importance of building a trusted partnership with an external provider. If you have this, then they can become your trusted advisors. Your HR team remains your expert on the technical aspects of the appointment, but your trusted advisors can lead the recruitment process for you.

Another option is to hire an independent specialist. I once ran a 2-year, 27-country campaign for senior executive talent on behalf of a client because they had an HR department but no recruitment expertise. I didn't supply any of the candidates, instead designed and ran the process, managed the external vendors and internal stakeholders and ensured the process ran smoothly.

There are a growing number of recruitment professionals who now operate as independent consultants and will literally work on site 'wearing the company' tie for maybe just one day a month, being the recruitment expert.

The worst mistake that companies make, particularly larger companies, is taking a member of their generalist HR team and making them the Head of Recruitment. In this situation, the best you can hope for, I believe, is a mediocre process that then gets enshrined in company doctrine and becomes the defacto way of doing things. The recruitment machine will work to the Club Sandwich level, and it may be the nicest Club Sandwich you have ever had, but it's not going to win a Michelin star.

Why does it matter? Because you aren't trying to be ordinary; you are trying to be extraordinary and create the best employer brand you possibly can.

By James E. Crawley

Chapter 14 – Ownership

If you are a small business, of say up to 20 people, then you are unlikely to have a full-time recruitment team or HR team, so lay the book down, go make yourself a cup of tea and come back in a minute when everyone has caught up.

Suppose you are a medium to large entity and have not only an HR department but also a recruiter or even a recruitment team. Your ownership talent acquisition is sorted then, isn't it? Well, probably not. I would imagine you think that ownership lies with the Head of HR or the Recruiter? You're wrong. Sure, they can own steps in the process or the mechanics of the process, but they can't own Talent Acquisition. Why is that? Well, it's simple. You or your key stakeholders own your brand and, therefore, also own your employer brand. As the guardian of that brand, you cannot pass off responsibility down to the depths of the organisation; it must remain at a strategic level.

I have met many talented internal recruitment professionals over the years who have been unable to fulfil their true potential to add value to the organisation because the senior stakeholders have taken little interest in the overall process. As a business leader, you must own that process, by all means delegate tasks but ensure that everyone in the organisation knows whose hand is on the tiller.

Often the reason senior leaders give me for not being so involved in the process is that they are too busy with their days jobs. Well, a) that isn't an excuse – remember the previous section on the true costs of recruitment, and b) that just tells me you haven't delegated correctly.

One of the most successful campaigns I ever ran was for a client who had 15 senior requirements across multiple geographies. Rather than hand it down to his country leadership team (who ultimately were going to make the hiring decision), we decided to keep the whole process centralised. This efficiency led to quick processing through the early stages of the process and, ultimately, the strong candidate buying in to the proposition. How much time commitment did that take? About 30 minutes once a week on a call with me. As everyone knew that the regional leader was tracking the progress on a weekly basis, things happened, and the recruitment campaign was prioritised in everyone's to-do lists.

One final point however, if you do hire true Talent Acquisition (not HR) Professionals then Empower them properly. Too often I see recruiters who are powerless to fix a broken process because the "are only a manager". These are your professionals, it doesn't matter if they are lower down the salary scale. When you pop round to your GP you don't tell him how to fix your health just because he is driving a hatchback and you are driving an Aston Martin.

Really good recruitment professionals within an organisation know how to say no, know how to demand the information and feedback they need from the business. If this is not happening in your business then you need to either re-educate your stakeholders or upgrade your team.

Chapter 15 – Good People Are Leaving. Is My Employer Brand Broken?

If you haven't yet created your employer brand, the simple answer is possibly yes. If, however, you have followed the steps above, the answer quite possibly is the opposite.

Let's think about why employees leave an organisation.
- They are unhappy with the organisation;
- There is a lack of progression or career development; and
- You are undervaluing the resource.

Employees can be unhappy with the organisation for a variety of reasons. they might have ethical concerns about the activities of the company; they might disagree with the company's policies or the way it treats people; they might just be bored having worked there for a long time. If you want to listen to your employees, hold regular engagement events with your staff; then you really shouldn't face such issues very often.

If there is a lack of progression or career development, it sounds negative, but it could actually just be the reality. Your company can only grow at the pace your market can accept, and it may be unrealistic to constantly provide greater challenges and better career opportunities for people. If employees are leaving because they are good and need progression, then it should be viewed as a success and celebrated. You should account for the fact that you have developed this individual to the maximum potential you can and now you are celebrating their growth and the fact they are moving on with your blessing. This proactive celebration of someone leaving tells other employers it's all right to grow themselves and develop themselves because they will leave with a lasting favourable view of your organisation, and you never know when you might meet them again!

Chapter 16 – Three Pillars of Creating a Killer Employer Brand

First, you don't need to engage the services of M&C Saatchi to create a killer employer brand. Sure, larger companies trying to reach a larger pool of potential talent can enhance their reach by increasing spending and getting their message to a wider audience, but guess what? If you haven't completed the basic steps that every organisation should, then your message can be flung as far and wide as you like, but it won't make any difference.

Now this book has covered the employer brand topic from several different angles, but it has focussed on the recruitment process. It will come as no surprise to you, therefore, that the first pillar in creating a killer employer brand is:

Getting Your Process Right

The second pillar relates to the fundamentals of the brand itself. You need a very clear definition of what your core values are, what your culture is, what your CSR agenda is, what your attitude to environmental issues or political issues is. I call this:

Getting Your Message Right

The third pillar is how your company operates. Do you offer flexible working hours? Do your offer job share? Is equity available? I call this:

Getting Your Proposition Right

There are whole books written on creating an employer brand, but it's really simple at its core. You are who you are, either celebrate that or change that but don't try and disguise that.

Chapter 17 – Conclusions

Employer brand is a very tenuous concept. It's hard to measure. Sure, you can do polls, and there are plenty of 'Best Companies to Work For' in every imaginable category. That doesn't actually make it any easier to recruit because even if you are number one, it still means there are 10 other organisations close enough to you to make similar claims. Don't mix up 'Best Company to Work for' with employer brand. 'Best Company to work for' is your marketing team's wet dream – better for selling to clients than prospective employees.

Employer brand is subtly different. It's about respect for the individual throughout your business processes, particularly recruitment. It's about doing things significantly differently than the way your competitors do. It's about bucking the perceived wisdom.

I came across a company recently, https://www.hiyacar.co.uk/, which is a peer to peer hire car company. When they are recruiting someone at the offer stage, they offer them a month's salary to walk away from the role rather than accept their offer.

I can't think of a better way to test a potential employee's motivation. The point is, they are doing something that no one else is; therefore, they have become a more attractive employer because they are creating a buzz around their recruitment process. They are creating a unique employer brand.

When Apple launches a new product, it is widely anticipated and pretty much sold out before it even hits the shelves, certainly before the purchaser gets their hands on he device to try it out. There is no reason why your company can't create such anticipation for new roles you create.

Now, you might think that I am only talking about large multinational businesses and their most exciting roles. I'm not. This could be applied to a local business just as easily.

A long-term client of mine leads a telephony and business outsourcing business, Webhelp, which has several large call centre sites around the UK. They have a constant demand to fill what many people might consider mundane 'call centre' roles. These roles are typical first jobs for people whilst they discover what direction they want their careers to take; therefore, there is a quite high turnover of staff through no fault of the company. The only way they can keep recruiting in such high numbers is to the best employer in the area and have the best employer brand they possibly can. This isn't achieved by paying above the market rate; they pay in the upper quartile, but it's still in line with the market standards. They achieve this by offering a fun interesting environment and a professional, slick recruitment process.

Ignore employer brand at your peril. You might not notice the repercussions in the short term. Matters might get trickier in the medium term, but they will become impossible in the long term. At that point, you will be paying above market rates for average talent that has very little emotional investment in your organisation.

If you don't believe what I have said in this book, then ask yourself this. Why does the Walt Disney Company have a Talent Acquisition Marketing department? I would suggest that no one knows branding like Disney knows branding.

I will leave you with my favourite, if not much over used, quote, attributed to many sources. I started using it in 1998, so I think I have as much as claim as any.

> 'If you are not the lead Husky, then the view never changes'.

Printed in Poland
by Amazon Fulfillment
Poland Sp. z o.o., Wrocław